What the Moon Gave Her

christi steyn

Andrews McMeel
PUBLISHING®

Andrews McMeel Publishing
a division of Andrews McMeel Universal
1130 Walnut Street, Kansas City, Missouri 64106

www.andrewsmcmeel.com

22 23 24 25 26 JST 10 9 8 7 6 5 4 3 2 1

ISBN: 978-1-5248-7382-0

Library of Congress Control Number: 2022934741

Editor: Patty Rice
Art Director/Designer: Diane Marsh
Production Editor: Brianna Westervelt
Production Manager: Chadd Keim

ATTENTION: SCHOOLS AND BUSINESSES
Andrews McMeel books are available at quantity discounts with bulk purchase for educational, business, or sales promotional use. For information, please e-mail the Andrews McMeel Publishing Special Sales Department: specialsales@amuniversal.com.

to my two grandmothers

my lunar guides

thank you for holding the moon for me

your birth happens more than once

chapters

the way of the waves

chapter one

Birth by the Ocean

an awakening

help me moon

there is nothing more that i can mortally do
but i still feel at fault even though
i did not ask the sun to set
there is nothing to grab onto
watching it sink, knowing that these hands are not fireproof
forget the reach
i've prayed for wings enough
made deals with the dark
none accepted, greeted with laughs
help me moon
find me soon

become a waterfall

please allow yourself to live
don't let it pass by
consume sky
you can be present
as long as there is music
there is dancing
spread as much light as you can
hold every hand
you will be on the receiving end my friend,
the rain falls and pours
but will always arrive back with the clouds
become a waterfall
be unbearable
be too much
be a whole heap of love

waving at waves

being honest with yourself is brave
you, my darling
can avoid this feeling of guilt
i have seen you lie in front of the waves
inviting them to wash over your skin
so you can begin,
begin to move on with this time we call life
you want to feel less heavy and i understand
your lies have now become sand
too much and scattered
fitting in never really mattered
why are you scared of being different?
i cannot grasp why you would kill the most interesting part
  of yourself

what the ocean gave her

you cannot expect me to fit in
when i breathe a different air
telling me to find you there
beneath the trees
somewhere among an autumn breeze

i am living in summer
with my lover, the ocean
my hope and guide
will never rely on someone to provide
it has always been the sea for me
stop convincing my heart to trust you instead
if it weren't for the sea
i'd be gone
i'd be dead

big sister baby
(a poem for mika koraal)

hello there, little girl
with a tiny pearl heart
coral is your name
the ocean swimming in your veins
today is only the start, we hear the beat of your jellyfish
  heart
innocent, ethereal mika
made from love and salty, blonde curls
i look forward to all the twirls on the kitchen floor,
i'll be your dolphin and you'll beg for more trips on my
  shoulders
we'll dive through oceans and climb choppy boulders
i'll be your mermaid in the pool and your mother,
my sister, will stare and drool
at the little creation that she made
with your dad
it started as a little grain of sand
an empty oyster
idea at hand
morphing with lobster and glee
now poseidon's greatest key

a fine place

there are truths tucked away inside
all of us
whispering how we are wrong
you do not need so many things
do less
more
is more stress
monstrously devouring your sense of calm
bring back ease
become a breeze
you are rushing only to rush somewhere
while you are already there
exactly where you need to be,
breathe into simply being
here is a fine place to exist

an opening

here i am
vulnerable in front of the universe
here is my heart
it will remain open for my time
in this body
i promise to pour love on everything like thirsty flowers
open to give
open to receive
please let me drown in this messy madness of being
and forever becoming

just a second, i am turning into gold

i am not available right now
it is time to take care of me
and my brave body
i will return more golden
my birth from the ocean

let me be alone
and meet my true home

curious little seahorse

find your calm
here, on the run
life is numb when you forget how to breathe
for ocean's sake, leave the racing at the door
flush the rush away
sway sway sway
in the river, little seahorse
don't swim upstream
the current flows towards a moonbeam
enjoy drifting your course
trust the water, little seahorse

and i will walk away stronger

with this broken organ of a heart
head high as the burning sky
i won't look back
with tears in these eyes, you do not deserve to see my pain
why do i crumble for someone who proved i am disposable?
i should feel nothing
i should despise you
i am angry that i still want to love you
but there is no going back
we are past the point of no return
watch me run
i'm already part of the brilliant sun

petals, balls of plasma, and a purple fin

i tried to be a flower
but never turned to face the sun
the moon has better melodies
so i prefer to sing with her

i tried to be a star
bad idea
they are too fast
burning in billions
and these things are all over the place

i tried to be a mermaid
help me find one first
to teach me how to breathe
underwater
dolphins don't take my request seriously

if i cannot breathe
everyone will tell me how i was wrong
how nothing magical exists
now i am trying to be human
settling for whatever sanity looks like
praying for petals, balls of plasma, and a purple fin

hello wind, can i get a ride?

you do not need to know what you are doing
i too have floated in wind long enough to bump into a
   blossom tree
grabbing branches can bruise your hands
make sure the tight grip is worth the burn
petals fall down and you will be left with naked bark
we are allowed to love the bare
there is beauty in being stripped
born again
do not worry about your birth
it happens more than once
welcome all change
only the skeptics trade in stagnancy
and your apology
is as heavy as breath
it is not needed to flow
allow yourself to let go

i need to scream my face off

there are moles crawling all over my head
gnawing on everything i said
eleven minutes
is all it took

eleven minutes
and i threw a book,
smashed my hand into this hairy carpet,
i have been shedding, stress combined with a zit

i am losing it
my sadness is driving me mad
i cannot feel myself
recognising nothing
bad
bad
to bed, to bed

slim thick

some parts should be skinny, and others must be full, the
  face symmetric, not anorexic unless you're talking about the
  belly
that should be flat, but below the back,
it should be all jelly, the butt can wiggle, but when the arms
  jiggle,
drop and give me six, the legs should not be sticks,
and not too thick, and cellulite is social suicide
another feature you have to hide
where is your thigh gap?
it's best you skip that nap
better to ride a bike, a ten-mile hike, become the one boys
  like
round breasts on your chest, with smooth skin, the recipe
  for a win
we don't like thin,
and we don't like fat and when you have acne, stay in your
  habitat
the stars on your face are undeserving of embrace
it needs to be fixed,
we have our values mixed

learning to inhale the ocean

you are tired of forgetting how to breathe
and my methods never seem to help
meditations and ocean impersonations are not your forte
but they make sense to me
for i am the one who inhabits the sea
never scared of learning her dance
you could have followed along
a teacher of tides
but i cannot be your breath, neither air, nor sky
as much as i would like to try after you called me *heavenly*
an angel, i am not
you can find me in the water

let the ocean wash over you

bursting with a fresh start
baptised into beginnings
the sea has a heart
filled with false dreams
pumping salt to heal wounds so bitter and bruised
the sharks would not dare to taste
you will cause the world to drown in your pain
there must be a way to wash it away
urchins will dissipate on sand
when you sting your hand, the blood is fast
the only demon holding on is
past
therefore it is gone,
no need to run but to the water here
flush it out of existence
and rinse from ankle all the way to ear

handle with care

"love handle" is a beautiful name
we should handle each other with love
acne should be called itty bitty kisses
flabby arms: hug extensions
belly pouch: a kangaroo hybrid
stretch marks are tiger stripes
because we are sexy cats
cellulite will be known as leg dimples, or puddle cuddles
wrinkles are forehead smiles
and when you have bacne
you are simply becoming a tree
what you see
are seeds
and when you scratch them, they bleed

apologise

apologise to your body
your disgust, disgusts me,
your vessel carries your soul
your creativity
your thoughts
your laughter
your tears
and you can't even look at your body without judgmental
  eyes
i know it was not always like this
you were conditioned
to compare your size,
to stare with the male gaze in ways
that are so unfair
it makes me want to throw up

how to be born again without being a baby

do a unique interpretation of a sundance

actively try to break old habits by gulping down a bottle of
  berry juice each time you repeat them

talk to yourself as if you are a puppy
hug your elbows,
close your eyes and repeat after me,
"this is a cocoon and when i open my eyes, i will be a butterfly"

open your eyes, and flap your new wings

envision bright purple in the center of your heart,
let it spread all over your body,
don't be scared when you start levitating

now do the moon dance,
you know the choreography
and she always joins in

searching for keys

i've slapped life through the face a couple of times
said *i'm giving up on you*
slammed the door
threw the key into rivers
i have walked away
given up
only to sit with myself
piled on pillows
wondering about my path
and why it lead me
here
in these moments
i find salvation in the paths not taken
the choices that have yet to awaken
and that thought allows me to get up
jump into water
search for the key
and say to life
i'll give you another chance

self taught

i have a burning desire
to inspire
as much as i can,
i continuously preach positivity and self love because it is
    something i desperately need
i feed people with affirmations and hope,
while neglecting my own ability to cope
i foster self hate in my mind
a fraud, imposter
unkind
i can't seem to reach the problem in my soul
i'm looking deep, but my heart is blind
practice what you preach
you filthy mind

the perspective of light

i spoke with a mountain today
and he taught me his ways
now i am learning how to be alive
by standing still
taking in where i am, finding light in dark places
until i am aware of my hands
the motion
and ability to feel
sensitivity is my superpower
and i will stay soft
not like some feathery fluff toy you get to punch
but like a cloud, gentle to the world
yet immune to wounding
treating distasteful hate
like condensation
i will always choose the light

a conversation with my tears

are you happy now that you are free?

i am never free, but always inside of you, my water proves that
  you are alive and capable of creating

creating tears?

yes, tears
and cleansing your darkest thoughts

when does it start to work?

do you feel lighter?

perhaps,
why?

after waterfalls there is light
i ask again,
do you feel lighter?

yes, you win

i want to be like the rain

the sky breaks down
mimicking me once more
i am not as dramatic as the clouds
creating thunder
pouring down with trembling drips and drops
the wind is not ashamed either
physically exerting every ounce of strength

i am jealous of her ability to unleash
especially with this inner scream smoldering inside
blazing, nonetheless
i have a silent approach
quiet tears falling through from upper arms to fingers
swallowing my pain
resenting the rain

you have you

after all this time
you finally found the calm
in isolation
what started as a dream
a soft hand reaching over your chest
to carry your moon cheek
tracing a smile
finally appreciation
something other than pure frustration
you are met with kind eyes
and feel deserving
you are worthy
and believe it
something changed your mind
someone changed
someone who will do anything for you
just listen
that someone has to be you

condensation

i am trying to persuade the clouds
i know they are made of magic
how else are they flying?

i am trying to persuade the clouds
by creating my own
take my tears from crying

i want to be a cloud
and go back in time
to when i was a child

make me a cloud
i will be reborn
to a time that i truly smiled

clouds don't do that apparently
they cannot reverse
but they give you dripping, drops of rain

clouds don't do that apparently
it is not a curse
they imbue you with streams again

perhaps there is hope

you can try and aggressively rip out the emptiness
i have tried creating explosions from a place of numb
there are days i only feel alive when swimming in ice water
i swear i cannot feel these hands,
but there is blood working
to keep me alive, if
my body fights for me,
i must be worth saving
perhaps this is the only convincing that i need
this cold, atlantic sea
this blood, we do bleed
beating bodies
there is so much breath
i cannot count them all
i cannot thank the air, how small
alive, with me and sadness and sea
tonight we wash with soap
this living body
reassuring me to hope

chapter two

You Plucked too Many Petals

leaving love

how can you love what you don't understand?

and when you told me
you don't know how to love me
because i am too much
as if i asked for anything
but mentioned my love language is touch
you say
you have no idea how to make me feel special
as if you are a penguin searching for a pebble
all i ever wanted was a space to be messy
to rip off the illusion of perfection i built so convincingly
and be dark
in front of you
i wanted to show you the raw parts too
where my sadness can be exposed
but you were too focused on being perfect
which is the exact thing i have been escaping
i wanted
to be painfully real
and to reveal my truest form
my mind is a chaotic storm
that you'll never get to know
you refused to explore
and chose to let go

it was all in my head

i keep replaying you in my mind, a fabricated fairytale
your eyes lit up whenever you saw me coming
i must have imagined the whole thing
you loved every part of me and wanted to take me in, that's
  what you said,
of course it was all in my head
my eyes were lying when they locked with yours
too blue to blink
even our breaths would dance in sync
when we held each other with tied up limbs through nights,
  becoming rope
i was clearly dreaming or creating hope out of thin air
i guess you weren't there, it was all a story that i invented
thanks for playing along, you only pretended

i want her back

you want to know why it is so hard to let you go
i will not speak in poetry for this but be blatant
i changed with you, and for you
now there is a version of me that i will never get back
that sunshine girl is gone, now fluent in rain language
grieving someone who is still alive like thunder
memories surrounding me like heavy clouds and the flashes
  hurt
i do not want to be betrayed to be stronger
i want her back
i want myself back before you

change is the only truth

if they didn't love you
like they promised

choose the wind
to guide you

from now on
you will learn
to trust the unpredictable
for there is no other truth
than change

and we carry on living beyond the light

and when they leave
you let go
with no tears, no crying, we do not ask them to stay another
   day
after a sunset there is darkness, but it doesn't take long to see
   the sunrise
it may even be more beautiful than before
and you will find that the light is bright
and love is soft and safe
you will adore the sun in different forms
it doesn't come from one source
you will find that even at night there is light
plenty of stars that guide
and you will find
that you are found, and never gone
only a reminder, to look beyond

goodbye

i loved you, hard
and when i love, **i love**
i smother
i
i told you
i told you this
i won't miss a kiss
and this is what i need and
you agreed
said
our love was guaranteed
so i made space to feel
and even though it wasn't real
it was beautiful while it lasted
i will eventually move past it
but this hurt is unbearable
nothing to do but cry
you're not my love
goodbye

all my loves

there is guilt
when heartbreak leaks into art
it was not my conscious decision to turn this pain
into a creative vision
with sonnets, and song and
you do not have to believe me
i too, am done convincing myself of this innocent execution
the subconscious loves a performance
do it for the craft
pulling pieces from the self into a large amulet
to be accepted as a virtuoso
a prodigy if i may
gather round gather round
arms wide open for the damaged, the oversharers,
the heartbreakers
gifted they call me
and the tears roll
i am an artist

**look me in the eyes and tell
me that you love me**

i have problems with your promises
they have become empty
the shooting stars are satellites
and the wolf is too fat for sheep's
  clothing
sweet something to nothing
ring and
no one is there
not even
eye swear

light can be deceiving

there lives an interesting space in this heart
that i carved for you
with quivering fingers
i knew that something wasn't right,
but from the start you only promised light
knowing how much words mean to me
the girl in love with poetry
i fell too quickly
when you told me you cared
trust is nicer than always being scared
i was done believing love is cursed
tired of always being hurt
in the end
it wasn't too confusing
i was only a fool
worth fun and using

can i be drunk instead?

pillows on the couch
the aftermath of that fight
last night was not a dream

today feels like one

trying to piece these scattered
thoughts
together

the worst hangover does not include boozing
if only it were that easy
i wish to be intoxicated
to forget

how is this your life?

when the moon is high and moths flutter in your throat
notice when they reach your heart
a reflux of words
the cat eating your tongue
how did you get here?
i know you feel trapped
please know, you can escape
allow yourself
you have to do this

my dream argument

in my dream we are holding hands
gentle talks
you don't sleep on the couch
instead of talking louder
over each other
the softest voice wins
clear
not condescending
it ends in hugging
not kissing
too cliché
we are aware when one of us is too emotional to speak and
  welcome
space and
time to process
we can walk away
but we stay in the same bed

i am not better than you, but i am better without you

i have gotten used to being alone
i don't want your plastic water anymore
i want to float on a cerulean lake
humming tunes i invented
smelling waves lightly scented
sweet salt with a hint of sweat
i drink from waterfalls
stop bringing me sugared soda
my brain is in a swelling pool of theories
expanding in the understanding of humans
i could hug them all now
and you don't feel the same
won't even pronounce their name
thanks for bringing this to me
but you can keep your english tea

time does not heal time

stop telling me time will heal everything
i know that
i know that in time my pain will fade away
but all these feelings will stay
stop telling me to wait
to feel okay
to feel anything
that doesn't work on me
i am addicted to living presently
in the now
right here, but i cannot do that
time is all i can taste
none left to waste
on someone undeserving of
my love
my body
my everything

in another life

i taste our morning coffee again
your arms become my daily den
i hear one of my 42 nicknames
we share stories round campfire flames
you nuzzle up to my cheek
i miss the way you speak
in another life
i take you for granted
but still feel enchanted
in another life, i don't know what i'm missing
in another life, i hope we're kissing

mind and body battle

you kissed my face
i froze in place
with nothing but you on every thought
forgetting love cannot be taught

there are only distractions to divert
i think of you,
and see hurt

as my brain is trying to talk
my muscle memory forgot how to walk
perhaps i need a crutch
i only feel your touch

love is all i know

if only i did not want love
desperately
i would be able to float through days,
without longing for lust
the desire to hold or be held
a desire to be desired
i know it tortures my mind
because i have felt love
and loved too much
knowing what i have lost
creates an all-consuming pain
we do not mourn what we never had
how could i not ache for love
the love i almost had?

there are secrets

i have shared
with past people
that crawl up on me
late at night and i awake
in a sweat of stress
disappointed i confided
too easy
me with all this trust and
overflowing hope for goodness
i don't have any wings
neither did they
now i create a cage
and keep them that way

your fire is one-sided

and to tell you the truth
i didn't think when i called you tonight
that it would be the last time we ever spoke
with my recent memory of you
how you woke
sleepily next to me and i inhaled your skin
it ended before we could even begin
if you asked me what i wanted
it would be for the seed to be planted
a lot slower
but you smothered it with water and too much light
you decided to dive
it made you feel alive
i have been drifting from the start
but you chose to skip the next part

bring back the sun i beg of you

we met with eyes
spoke in lullabies
how soft we were to touch
a person cannot love this much
there is not enough breath
for days to love left
i want all the time with you
relive every rise and fall of the sun's view
your name is never spoken but sung
i beg of you
bring back the sun

only the moon as a friend

i have been waiting for you on the moon
my arm getting tired of reaching out
it really is heavy not carrying a single thing but sweet
  nothings and empty promises
hiding all the blemishes is easy
your kisses never leave an imprint on my face
but i still remember every ounce of embrace
here i am again
with only the moon as a friend
carrying a new hope, with a wish and a star
the weight is less
knowing you won't travel this far

open your eyes you are not flying

for a moment in time
i had you,
called you mine
boy of sunshine
blind was i
there is no sky
where lovers meet
for i opened my eyes
and found ground on my feet

when we broke up

the sun hated me
it was either burn or a game of invisibility
nowhere to be seen
when we broke up
i felt too numb for crying to be done
staring at objects for way too long
when we broke up
the clouds that used to form paintings above our eyes, only
   became clouds
the canvas, only skies
sounds became harder to bear
i heard screeching everywhere
when we broke up
i tried to hate you, but only hated loving you
when we broke up
i didn't split a meal in two
we've broken up, so take care
i'll take myself everywhere as i am, complete
turns out the sun was always my heartbeat

i stack the pillows next to me to
pretend that you are still here

the clouds mean more to me

i gave you clouds
to share
and you took my rainbow with none to spare
leaving nothing but rain
your umbrella is not effective
stop using open fingers to catch tears
when my smile disappears
don't fake surprise
i see it in your eyes
there was never a care for what i had given
you only see a cloud
but they are my heaven

the glistening stone

i will eventually stop missing you
even when i am filling space with other people
they make me feel more alone
you were my one true home
for a moment i never wanted to move
it was only you
among all the stars
and fish in the sea
and sand on the beach
you were the glistening stone i wanted to pick and keep
now i have to throw you back into the ocean
and watch you skip
over boulders of liquid salt
soon to be swallowed by
waves
and spit out again for someone else to find
and keep
that glistening stone
it cannot be my home

i will grow wings to fly away from you

i am done with your half love
when my happiness drove you to madness,
 i knew my wings had to grow stronger
courage was needed to get the hell away from you
it was never going to be easy
freedom never is
when you are taught to focus on shiny bars
but the only cage i need are these ribs
i hold myself
tucked into salt curls and tired limbs
made of love
and you can't convince me otherwise

the stars between us

it started when you stopped talking to the stars
and laughed when i said you felt far
as you began to lose wonder
i danced with thunder
grabbing hands with rain and hail
come sail with me
pleadingly
pulling you towards the sea
but you forgot how to swim,
forgot how to fly
forgot we could travel through sky
stop asking how
stay on earth for now
i will transport without you next to me
it is sad to be more happy
alone, with the cosmos
i miss the old you the most
but it's time to go
i'll tell the stars you said hello

i still shiver when someone says goodbye, because
i have felt permanence in those words

there will be no begging tonight

when you leave
that door will remain closed
and your footprints will no longer be
imprinted on my heart
but in the sand,
ready to wash away
any day now
the moon is already closer,
forcing her tides to rise

getting out

let me sleep when i want to sleep,
this cage is enough
insomnia enforced
i am taking back my life
call me dramatic
call me dramatic again
call me crazy
i am ready to fly away
from you
and i cannot wait

my mask is from mars but i am not a star

how i have tried to communicate with eyes
only to find our hearts filled with different stories
i grow mad
i go mad with near distance
how can one feel so far while being held?
i've always known you were a star
believed i could become one too
believed i could be placed right next to you
underestimating the exhaustion of pretending
is my mistake
i am a fake
for i do not belong in the sky
i am sorry, for convincing you i could fly

chapter three

How to Grow Wings

-in the cocoon
-butterfly burst

in the cocoon

i am addicted to forgetting the world

shutting down while looking at flowers
don't you dare interrupt me
i walk far because i have not heard enough songs
there will never be time for all the music

i wish i was a dragon

i am an anxious apologiser
i am too polite
preaching kindness like my new gospel
it is my only light
i look at beautiful things for too long,
because i feel it in my blood
like a mantra song

so when you call me *fake*,
i take an arrow to the core
it is my being,
being seen as *trying* once more

yes

it's happened before and i try to forget certain events
and i resent your opinions
because the lesions on my heart go unseen
to the normal eye
and my smile doesn't work when i want to cry
calling me sensitive,
well that won't help either
cause i'm a growing tree,
not a fire breather

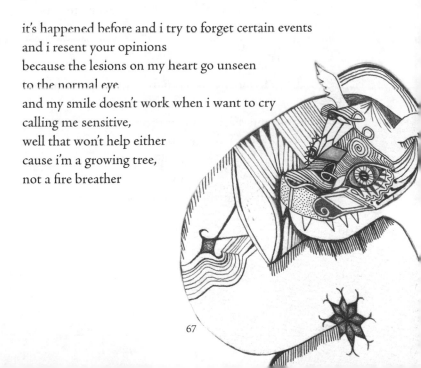

you don't have to escape your sadness

perhaps that is why they keep coming back
   so often
being suppressed is not freeing
it's claustrophobic and causes one to panic
allow your sadness to burst in absolute
   ecstasy
make whale calls
fountain the ocean from your eyes over the
   bodies of seven mermaids
unleash that inner turmoil
volcano to the moon
there is no shame feeling
listen to your sadness,
they may turn out to be wiser than you
   think

cocoon days

i am learning to love myself
on unlovable days
i allow myself to go slow
choosing kindness instead of judgment
i won't hate myself for not being happy
some days are for sadness
and when sadness comes
i expose my heart and ask her to talk
what can i do for you?
you are safe here
you are safe here
i know how exhausting joy can seem
she will appear again
soon, without trying
there is nothing wrong with you
there is nothing wrong with you

becoming ghosts

i catch myself
making excuses for other people
when being ignored
locked out
uninvited
but deep down my smirking insecurities are pointing
   straight at me
pathetic little fool
can't even hold on to friends
people always leave and i'd rather hold the door open than
   be labeled as "needy"
let them go about the business of
ghosting
while becoming ghost
feeling no light through this translucent body
i want them to love me
i hate this wanting and this waiting
and this pretending to be strong
as if they did nothing wrong
the game we like to play with our emotions tucked away
but you won't catch me
begging for anyone
who doesn't choose to stay

how to train the air to stop choking me

melancholy has become my mantra
and i am not proud
this summoning is a default i try to reset
i regress to sadness in these sheets
bleeding boredom and staring at
ceilings
my eyes feel rutted textures
pitted with paint
longing for feeling
out of my reach
we meditate again tomorrow
the healing will come
once the breathing is done

christmas away from home

i don't even want to write about this
it makes me uncomfortable
and it doesn't feel like christmas
and i don't really feel like christi
christimas is dead
that little girl who couldn't go to bed the previous night
and jumped on everyone's bed singing christmas songs
struggling to gather the troops before opening their gifts
how lucky if i can get them together before church
that is the memory
not this christmas
this christmas doesn't count
neither does my birthday
please do not get me wrong
i am beyond grateful
and guilty for my sadness

every phone call on sundays with my mom

hello mamma,

i know we haven't spoken in a few days, i am so sorry, i
know it is my fault, i didn't want to answer and cry because
i know it worries you when i do that, this is not an excuse, i
sincerely hope it isn't, but i have come to the conclusion that
i am a skilled manipulator, so who knows when i am telling
the truth, i love you, promise me you will not worry about
me, your new dog is so beautiful, my apartment is too small
to have a dog, but i have four fish (at the moment), they die
easily, i have managed to keep one plant alive for six months,
she sleeps on the windowsill behind my bed, because it is
the only window that works, how do you keep your flowers
alive? i feel like i am cleaning all the time, listen, if everything
fails, can i come home and you take care of me again? when i
come back to south africa, i need to sleep without worrying
for twelve days and then i will be able to start seeing people,
i have too much that i want to do, yet i am doing nothing,
i promise tomorrow will be better, i promise i will not cry
tomorrow

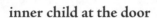

inner child at the door

your heart knocks on your chest
and pleads for a gentle caress
now
covering your ears
won't do a thing
because your inner fears
are a constant ring
when you leave it hanging
your inner child starts banging
against the gates and you forget the meaning of
stillness
start treating your mind as an illness

"what is wrong with my biology?"

little you needs an apology
hug your shoulders, whisper to your heart

"today we begin with a tender start"

social anxiety through the eyes of an extrovert

arriving at the event after planning the look, taking the subway,
  dodging the rain, the people, the noise, reminding yourself to
  breathe
as you get there, you have to match the energy
oh my goodness how are you i am so happy that you are here babe
  you are looking incredible come now give me a hug give me give me

you failed, they immediately ask you what's wrong
are you not having fun
listen it's your favourite song

the commute was a little intense, you say pointing at the rain
surely this excuse will do, but eyes of confusion follow you
should i sit down
give the wine
sorry i see you are drinking red instead
find red wine and open it with the *turning thing*
great you can't even speak, think of something to say, one thing
can you think of one thing to say idiot
i need the bathroom
i don't but i do
who are you
mascara looks smudgy
breathe in
breathe out
smile

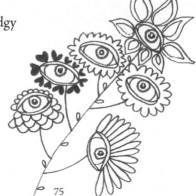

hands and names
(the last memories of my grandmother)

i wish i drew your hands
my last memory that i have,
i was holding them
soft, gentle flesh,
you could not speak
it did not matter

we had touch
dementia cannot take
  away your sense of feel grandma and
touch is the language of the world,
that and art of course

i do not like drawing hands
i am lazy, and have not practiced
always prefer to crop paintings at the shoulders
putting hands behind head or
an elaborate bouquet of flowers

i remember your hands, because it was hard to
  look at your face,
and see you search for my name

let me kiss you instead

isolation

there are days when
i feel too guilty to talk to people
i see their perfect pictures
picked specifically
for me to envy
through a screen
and feel unworthy

i have made friends with nature
being elevated by the trees,
they understand my silence
the wind whispers to me
"you are not alone"
"you will be a part of something big"

do not get me wrong
people do notice me
of course they do
i am crying in the streets of new york
and my mask does not cover my entire face

self-help sunflowers

when i can't help myself
i help others,
so when you see me carrying sunflowers,
show me a spot in the light,
a place where they can bloom
where everyone will see them
and everyone will say,
"wow, those sunflowers are so beautiful"

what a moment

i put them there

to the man who's never cried before

let it flow through
the apologies you never got
the times you were told to toughen up
losing family or love you thought was real
please know it's beautiful to feel
sometimes there are only tears
to complement our inner fears
let it flow through
when there are no words to speak
goddammit
it doesn't make you weak

do you ever just want to

stand on a sunny corner
of the bustling manhattan streets
and take in the sun
listen to a beautiful song
type something in your notes
look at people go about their day
no questions asked
just go
i'll go
i will keep going
and before you even know it
you are growing
please call me
tree

we try again tomorrow

face planted in knees
fed by tears rolling like streams

we try again tomorrow

with puddles at your feet
head numb from a pounding heartbeat

we try again tomorrow

even if you can't recognise your face, red
and you rotate from crying, food and bed

we try again tomorrow

i cannot fix this one thing

as a little girl, i was a creative engineer,
always turning blank corners into disneyland
a stuffed zebra connecting to my rainbow umbrella
postcards of florence cut out as a greenscreen for my barbie
  dolls
like a movie scene,
anything out of place, was easy to fix
just add the colour purple
i was convinced that i could make everything around me
  beautiful
my head knew stillness, the trampoline calling me to
  transport once more
the secret garden was limitless, i would continuously stare at
  the statues of gnomes

they never came to life

many moons later, here in my little square in new york
i cannot find my calm,
tears streaming like the rainbows i once knew
curious about my pain,
thinking and writing and fixing
conjuring up my grand plan
come now,
come now,
why so blue?
i cannot fix this one thing
no purple paint can fill me now

the markers have all dried up

82

my mother

i know you want to hold me,
and tell me how much you love me
you are nineteen hours away
"only two flights"
i keep reminding myself
like a personal mantra or coping mechanism
you told me, you make sense, christi
and that meant more than air
most of the time, i have absolutely no idea what i am doing

so if you see a beautiful, lioness lookalike sitting on a large
  rock somewhere in stellenbosch
that is my mother
and she is probably thinking about me
lucky girl

flowers in isolation

it seems impossible
to find light in a setting so gloom
but here is my little orchid ready to bloom

i've never been able to keep flowers alive
not once have i succeeded in sustaining
  another life
this flower, is my hope

it is my change and my chance
there will be brighter days past this pandemic

within, and further along the way
taking care of something is such a blessing
i should do it more often

in order to take care of others,
i need to take care of myself
us mothers
have an important job to do
yes, it is only a flower
but flowers are children too

a poem on being tired

or depressed or anxious or one in the same
i can't really tell the difference
except one makes your parents proud
the other makes you feel like an accident
what part you ask?
the number of times you blink in sync with your breath
or how many times you scratch your left shoulder
stop doing that it's turning red
maybe i should run
i find the idea of running so much more liberating than
   running itself
unread books in my library shelf
i lie
i don't have shelves of books
only one stack
a tower
held by a humidifier
and a dying flower
dead
the flower is long dead with only
a deep reek through the room it will spread
what a beautiful bookmark he will make
 a bookmark only to remind me that i didn't water my plant
i swore i would but i can't even take care of myself
bad mother
i whisper i whisper
as i drag myself to the sink

a poem for the monster in my head

i cannot hide from myself anymore
using poems to describe my insides
they are not as colourful as i hoped
but they are true
they keep whispering
this is you
my present seems to have paused
i don't feel like a wolf
therefore i must be a fraud
some days one cannot appear strong
or easy or still
constantly trying to rebuild
nothing times nothing is more nothing
numb is also the outcome of a sum
the end result of poetry
does not reveal a hero in me
some days it will
but it seems like my cup has spilled
i make life more difficult than it needs to be
i've never mastered simplicity
so fill this bowl with hot water instead
and drink the honey,
get out of my head

birds aren't born flying

you will feel hopeless
and scared
at the start of a new chapter
do not fight your courage because of uncertainty
you belong
we all learn by trying
birds aren't born flying
we fail, and fail
and fall
you simply have to do it
everyone starts off a hatchling
blinded by egg glue with sticky wings

what i want women to know

it is easy to say
take up space,

but hard to do if you have never been asked about your
  opinions

it is easy to say
just say no,

but difficult when you have been taught that being "wanted"
  is the greatest achievement

it is easy to say
stop caring about what others think
dress the way you want
love who you want
love yourself

but it can seem impossible when you have to heal first,
and unlearn all that you were taught
trauma can live deep inside bones,

take it slow
it is okay to be scared
just being is enough
you don't always have to be so tough

butterfly burst

let your wings grow

please
do not please everyone
you will fall short and resort to settling
and regretting
stings
when you are the one cutting your own
wings
dare to be daring
and ignore all the glaring from the crowd
nothing can make the scornful proud
and you don't have time worth wasting
you are tasting
life
the ones that matter are in awe
it's only you that they adore
be honest and show how you feel
i don't care if you are broken
at least you are real

if you cannot write poetry
write about yourself my dear
there in the lines
a poem will appear

happy to have you here

i heard from a nocturnal bird, that
the water is purple in heaven
therefore i started praying to sunflowers,
now i have stratos powers
yes, i can talk to the sky
clouds do not cry
they never say goodbye
we never leave or go away
part of this universe
is where we always stay

becoming rivers

it happened as effortlessly as imagination
there were stones in my head
hurting my neck
one can only be a solid rainbow for seven days
i was not lucid dreaming
reality has become *floaty*
here i am, drifting in the present
filled with fog,
now following a frog to his pond
come sit and hum natural notes
the earth will swallow you
letting go of the heavy is heavenly
finally, i am water

turning into a tree i see

i don't like who i am when i am upset
stop being silly
spilling tea is only funny when you can clean it up
get a mop and stop sulking
no one is going to save you
be capable
you and you and you
grow gracefully
learn from all the trees, go slowly
welcome change and phases
adapting always amazes you but it shouldn't
look how far you've come
you cannot see the roots
with a view this high
metamorphosis
from tree to sky

you have everything you need

i have been searching for the ultimate key
to fulfillment
what do i need to be more?
what elixir do i have to pour?
for reaching full potential
a celestial being of light
the answer is this
there is nothing to add
the list of requirements are mad
all you have to do
is lose that idea or version
you are complete
the expectations are obsolete

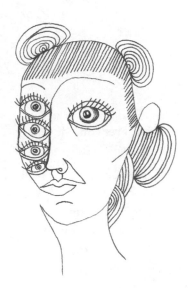

not everyone deserves to learn your water dance

abandonment feels really loud at times
especially to me
but in these times i go to the sea
to taste her greatness
my truth is this
wide with wonder
i will not settle for mediocrity
not with endless ocean showing me
there is no end to my ability to thrive
they have to make you feel alive
and loved to even stand a chance
otherwise they aren't welcome to water dance

my mother is a garden

my mother is a garden
with fauna fit for butterflies,
honeysuckle, lavender, wild peach, and malva
these flowers are
fueled by the tears of her children
she never needs rain
the garden works hard when we are sad
she sends the birds to sing us to sleep
vegetables enough for a feast
but still she is questioned
about the amount of sunlight
i cannot control the sun
she laughs

but my arms are trees
enough for shelter
and the air that my family breathes

26

my sixteen-year-old self had an entire shelf dedicated to
  your successes
was it three wedding dresses you wanted to flaunt at 22
and did the baby come before or after you became a
  billionaire
an actress of course, hopefully in a movie with a
  thoroughbred horse
you told people you wanted to be a doctor while fainting in
  biology
you made a promise to the moon, said, "see you" no
  knowledge of astrology
i didn't do too bad for us, but surprise, we still hate running,
  and focusing, and making phone calls, so look at this
young chris, we are not afraid of the unknown and we
  challenged ourselves to trust the process of growing
the more big decisions we make, the more big decisions we
  can make and don't take this the wrong way
but you think differently about a lot of things now
and i am so proud of your ability to change
we fear a lot less now, little one

beginning to become by being

look
let me be honest about where i am at
or where i find myself being
i am always becoming
like to think i'll always be humming
not some melancholy tune
i don't worship the moon only
i tend to feel more lonely than sprite
you say i'm bright but this girl has been
  dim
the problem within
i know these words cannot reach all
i know what it's like to feel small
to pain from the soul
what is whole?
an entire part
in this heart i feel shattered
brain scattered to piece together what
  i am meant to be
and by being, eventually, hopefully
i'll find me

you live in the sky

be happy when they don't understand you
make them frown
some people want to see you drown
but you are fluent in the language of your universe
and they have this curse
they can't speak to birds
or grow wings among other things
please don't think
you have to shrink
and fit in with these close-minded cacti
you aren't a mud person
you inhabit the sky

your friends are fairies

surround yourself with mythical creatures
friends who feel like roses
make life beautiful
soft and tough all at once
you deserve wonder
that's when you know you can fly towards the light
don't ever feel small
love, and adore, and glisten more

heavenly human you are overthinking
shut up you are perfect

you have layers to shed
from skin, born from head
darkness created out of air
unaware of your own destruction
damaging your thoughts and creation
let go of expectation
you are enough
part heaven
let out the light
we can't fear the bright
as part of the sun
you have begun

we all have butterfly tendencies

fluttering around, never finding the right flower
unable to sit down, unable to quiet the anxious
  voice telling us to keep going
we feel undeserving of rest, because there is
  always something else
always more and more to explore
we forget
wings can't fight wind forever
and there will always be more sky,
more space to fly
stop flapping, and look up,
you are not missing anything when wandering
  about
you don't have to figure it out
more time will arrive
we are so busy
we forget that we're alive

stop stepping on these wings / i will fly soon

what is happening to me
losing reality as i breathe autumn leaves
i float on walking fingers from coffee shop to coffee shop
not counting caffeine
planning life while never living
thrown by simple questions
with no answers
please stop staring
you're stepping on my wings
they are dusty
out of practice
at least i keep hope in my backbone
do not push me
let me wait for the wind to settle
let me wait for my tears to dry

listen to your dreams

attend to your imagination
those dreams are talking to you
try something new
escape being fake
take in all
and start a war against being static
i don't mind being dramatic
never have
i'm only asking
when did you become lifeless?
and miss all the aspirations you have been yearning
my love, start learning
your vision is waiting, dipped into truth and sealed with a
  wish
you won't flourish by following fish
you can't breathe underwater yet
but if you keep drawing that sunset
with all those colours in pen
you will transform into a heaven

the path of flight

after nurturing your imperfections
and answering questions
your new philosophy is tasting every breath
going steady is a necessity for your soul's being
when you try to take it in
you can hear birds sing
but won't learn to dance with them
won't learn the language of the song within
open each wing
sing sing *sing*

flying is hard with human hands
flying is hard when you have no plans
but it's the only way you can reach the sky

make a wish to yourself my star

when will you see the magic in your
  madness?
when will you realise the star you have
  been wishing upon
is not the sun, but a ray
living in your dna, yes there are wishes in
  your bloodstream
don't scream,
become a dream
and stop the fear
even stars someday,
will disappear

moon snake

you call me shape shifter
i am a moon drifter
going through phases of shed and birth
my head won't stay on this earth
i will unzip in skies of space
the old me will erase
never forgotten
there is nothing rotten in change
embrace the new and the strange
you call me indecisive
always in crisis
my ecdysis is not from serpent
but from within
the sun slivers beneath my skin

chapter four

Dancing Dolphins

in strangeness we find our true selves

moss mush in my head

i like to pretend

i am a little piece of purple moss,
under a wise old tree
sun rays reach me here
through trunks and raging roots
a wide cage
easy to escape

i am warm
and small
and damp
and safe

my best friend is a golden retriever who brings me water
rain does not fall here
when i don't feel like talking
my friend understands
he pours the water from his mouth
i am good at absorbing liquids
and i can produce my own food through photosynthesis

he kisses me and caresses my leaves
in return
i give stillness,
i create calm
one day, i will be placed in a bonsai tree
and everyone will look at me and say,
"i love purple moss"

i like to pretend

**pretending to be a dolphin
can solve all your problems**

soothing binaural beats of song to
  calm your mind
envision the elision of all things blue
  and bind with every hue
negativity will shoot through your
  blow hole
and you can dive through the ocean
  like a water-mole
you wiggle with natural ease,
silky bodies that rub as they please
carefree
flying through the skies
with eyes glistening the truth
nostalgia of my youth

tears to toe

when you start crying
make the tears
reach your toes
because nails are seeds
and water makes them grow

how to love yourself

make humming noises
you have a sound place that allows you to babble brilliance
use it to whisper wonders
straight to the
core
speaking about the belly
hug it
squeeze it
feel the warmth
your body beats and bleeds for you
it moves and macarenas
magic
if you shame it
you harm the heart
be thankful and focus
on every part
'tis a miracle to even breathe
so leave all this fighting with the mind
it won't make you grow
so choose to be kind

how to make a tree smile

1. say "hi tree, let me give you a hug!"
2. hug the tree for five seconds
3. if you start crying make sure you use your eye water to feed the roots
4. give the tree a name and tell them why you think that name suits them
5. observe the movement of the tree and create a short interpretive dance routine to celebrate their existence
6. make wind sounds
7. thank them for being books and homes and pay attention to the birds or squirrels that they lodge
8. give up your darkest secret or something you feel guilty about

this will make you feel less heavy, remember to leave the tears with the tree

now you can float away as light as a leaf in the wind

feel better immediately

if you want to immediately feel better
it always helps to impersonate the colour yellow
in gibberish
bakachichiyoyeeekahshi
quickly pretend to be a koala
only the face
now grab a piece of eucalyptus
this is your invisible flute
make a magic whistle sound
ooooouuuuyyy
close your eyes and pretend a floating ship is calling to you
call back
rrrrhhhhaaaaa
there you will find a fire fish human
here to grant you wings or the power of speed
choose wisely

thumb tales

i feel lonely so i pinch the squishy part under my thumb
this flesh
warm
proving that i am alive
a lonely life at times, even around people, lonely
unsatisfied and questioned
why do you keep pinching your hand like that?

can i have another one?

i had too much to drink
because i stopped thinking about the world
the pending dreams
we talk about whales and i drown in your passion
becoming whale
and yes, i have been throwing this stick to your alsatian
she keeps bringing it back
i could do this forever and she will always bring it back

sunshine sins

the sun has a foot fetish
your sandals making him sweat
the g-string of the toes
makes lava drool out his nose

the sun also likes to binge
he's swallowing comets while swiping on hinge
hoping to be matched with a brand-new star
had enough with the moon for she lives too far

the moon is depressed

she spent every cent on a brand-new dress
to show the sun,
 for he can't caress her face
they both live in space but speed dating
is all they know, communicating by what they can show
done shouting across the world
she swirled to show her brand-new look
but the sun had a star that he betook
the moon tried to hide her despair
he kissed a star with her standing there
delightfully done, dressed to the nines
will never admit he dimmed how she shines

a star

spikes smother all that i am
reaching out to the abyss, a space acropolis
with nothing to touch
yearning for saturn's ring to surround me
a simple embrace i long for a comet's kiss on this faceless face
touch is all that i have
nothing to touch
the most important moment of my life
is the explosion

explaining blue to someone who can't see colour

i find no sadness in blue
labeled to describe mondays
how when the sky is so hopeful?
it is like
letting go of a secret
between you and the moon
that feeling when your body is covered by ocean,
it is seeing the first star of the night
or rubbing ice
light blue is a puddle and dark blue is stepping on a ship
but you don't know where you are going
and you don't really care
blue is calm
blue is a doctor telling you,
you're going to be okay
it is your first dance when you learn to sway
it is a stranger's concern when you cry on the subway
blue cares
blue has felt a lot and doesn't talk about it,
but blue knows what it's like to be alone, so you can trust blue

pretending to be flowers

it's not quarantine when you pretend to be a flower,
it's not quarantine when standing still is your superpower

if you don't drink water, you will definitely die,
if you can't find the sun, you must look to the sky

it's not quarantine when you pretend to be a plant,
it's not quarantine being served at the vegan restaurant

if you don't meditate and breathe, you will definitely die
if you contain thc, you will make people high

explaining yellow to someone who can't see colour

it is the wrinkles on your mother's eyes when she smiles
the little drop on the top of grass
it is the feeling of heat when you rub your palms
a child's laughter
the image of someone catching snow with their tongue
your grandfather's stories of when they were young
a pineapple ice smoothie with peppermint
and every time you squint while searching for sun

dancing in poetry

some moments feel like poetry
don't think about it too much
smile, and dance between the lines
the stanzas always have space for you
 to roll

explaining red to someone who can't see colour

whether you believe in love at first sight or not
this is the first kiss
something that exists outside of reality
that feeling you get when you reach the top of a mountain
surprising
it is losing yourself while looking at fire
red is opera, dirty dancing, and running in moonlight
red feels too much
it is heartbreak but also a lover's touch
red chooses passion
with a dash of wild

go to sleep

seeing stars have been keeping you awake
so take the moonpath less travelled
galaxies are dark enough to fall through
and you are pretending to sleep
but mary is better at counting sheep
no need to compete with blue blankets
orange will be fine
the sun will think you are his baby
and maybe he will leave you alone

a real summer's day

i long for the summer

tangled hair
the smell of sunscreen
sand on every single thing
how i long for the summer
burning feet
warm wind melting strawberry vanilla ice cream
as i eat
sun kissed cheeks
freckles on the nose
how everything glows
with air filled with ocean and laughter
as if nothing can go wrong now or hereafter

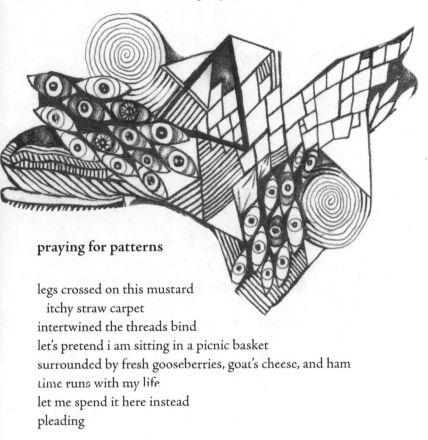

praying for patterns

legs crossed on this mustard
  itchy straw carpet
intertwined the threads bind
let's pretend i am sitting in a picnic basket
surrounded by fresh gooseberries, goat's cheese, and ham
time runs with my life
let me spend it here instead
pleading

time will not stop for me
the tasks,
towering, *overflowing*
left leg, now extending
counting hair is not productive
one to ten, again, again
feels so good on my mind
a pattern for me
i haven't seen a pattern in a while

how to escape the mind

briefly of course
jump on your made-up horse
give her a name like aphrodite
doesn't have to be god or a deity
envision the smell of a crisp-cut pear
gobble it on a wandering chair
or a brand-new pony, she loves to eat
is vegan right now so leave out the meat
choose a location, not earth, but far
your destination is a purple star
gallop away but skip the black holes
when you enter one, they're infested with trolls
the fourth dimension will feel like a crime
congratulations you can travel through time

my crow friend and i

a bird called on me today
and wanted to say
you look lonely
and i would know as a friendless crow
i told her no
just dreaming in sky
i envy how you fly
the bird thought i had feathers on my head
but chose to use it as a nest instead
i don't have wings
but i'll work through my sorrow

i have wings, said the crow
for a new friend to borrow

i prefer to be the odd girl

to be honest
i think being strange is the best
all these fancy people with their vocabulary and pseudo
  intellectual
biodegradable coffee pots
caffeine is not a personality trait
i prefer to escape
to float with silliness into the sky's abyss
let me lick your face and have a taste of your
wonderful
that sparkle of golden dust
there it is
like we discussed
keep the weird
and grow that glitter beard

i go to the dogs during dinners

you are mad
that i spoke to their dog for a long time
but between the wine and the cryptocurrency talks
i enjoyed the puppy obsessed with walks
he loved me for scratching and rubbing his ears
not for owning tesla shares
this corner of the party belongs to me
these furry friends aren't hard to please
give me a minute i'll be right there
of course i don't care
if i'm covered with hair

i don't care if you like my art
my soul likes my art
and my mother too

dance

the rules for being human are messy
here is a body
feed it
don't bump into other bodies too much
touch is lust
you are nature
water and blood and spicy mud
we all become stars silly
and you should be dancing right now

this poem

black on white
for a moment, becomes a part of me
my thoughts dragging through each line
continuously
perhaps you get to stay, little one?
little—
is not what i should call you
who knows
perhaps you live here longer than me
my eternal thought
where person becomes poem
creation, if i may

chapter five

Full Moon Bloom

live in your power

what the moon gave her

after she drowned in moonlight
her eyes changed to comets
possessing the power of black holes
she spoke in colour
but human ears are not fit for
rainbow talk or
intergalactic star walk

the moon gave the girl a curse
by understanding the universe
no one understood her
and sadly there was no cure

you are standing on a mountain already

we do what we can
not every day can be used to reach the top of the mountain
reflect on your progress and notice the lack of internal rest
we cannot keep sprinting to catch up with comparisons
your story is important
that beautiful life you keep judging
the finishing line moving further and
further away
the mountain is not growing my friend
you have been adding more rocks
calling it the castle from a dream
you are so high up it echoes when you scream
be aware of the
space
you have created
we do what we can yes,
but pay attention to all that is done
perspective will prove we've already won

hello doubt, do you want to eat me?

doubt comes in and sits at the fireplace
you do not fight it
openly allow it to steal your warmth

why do we encourage such robbery?

we are too polite with this imposter
permitting it to our beds
a widespread of insecurity
wailing in our heads

you will not eat me today, doubt
the plan was clever
you will not drink from my mind you fool
not now,
not ever

all hail the wild women

the ashamed
the banished
the wicked

being scolded by small minds
with little lives
you have not seen half of what she has
you have not discovered power
too pious to taste poison
i see

all hail the witches

the scorned
the burned
the gifted

they sang with eagles,
and slept with wives
you will not experience the life of a goddess
a haven of heathens

i don't want to be a good woman

i don't want praise for a cross-legged pose
i don't want to speak like a rose
i don't want to giggle when you touch my arm
i don't want to run from every alarm
i won't be scared and cover up
won't shiver when i say shut up
i said no, that means go
leave, i am not asleep
i see everything, as i stand
i am more than a ring on my hand
more than my body and beauty
raising children is not my duty
the good women left and found a choice
good woman, see, you have a voice

becoming a home

may you get drunk and have conversations with stars
may you feel how small you truly are
being insignificant is a gift
may you feel everything now
this breath with hand sweat adrenaline
may the urge for dancing be a deadly sin
more addictive than lust or greed
may you never need someone to hold at night
but may they hold you anyhow
elbows, hips, thigh dips,
you belong within
alone,
this skin
a home is what you were made to be
may you become
a sacred body

how to be invincible

(for this to work, please select five of the following steps
to become a unicorn with butterfly wings)

+ wear sparkly green eyeshadow
+ roll your r's unnaturally long (i am talking about the letter r)
+ read a book on a bench like a bush baby (one page minimum and yes this poem counts)
+ make distinct animal noises, i.e., dog, elephant, horse, gorilla, pig, lion, turkey, pterodactyl or whale
+ select your favourite leaf and thank them for producing air, that was really kind and they don't owe us anything; give the leaf a little massage and exhale some carbon dioxide to make them high and happy
+ draw a picture of your two favourite animals combined as one
+ think of a person you love and sing their name (this will send cheerful waves in their direction)
+ take a deep breath with your hand on your heart, this is your body, from now on you will practice being more kind to your body
+ do a little happy dance
+ wear two scrunchies anywhere on your outfit or limbs or hair, just do it!

you are about to touch the stars, don't look back

your higher self
your worth
your power
your space
your truth

is more important than being likable

say no
care less about what others think
take up all the space
and dance around
let them watch and let them talk
they'll never learn to fly

finding sunlight

the winter is so cold
patches of sun
are the new den
my little haven of rays
here on the corner in manhattan
my shadow stretched out long behind me
she is still here
reminding me that i exist

goddess you

if they laugh when you refer to yourself as a goddess
let them go
if they don't understand the way that you move
give them a show
people will always talk
and find fault in those that are free
keep flying
my golden one
let go
you're close to the sun

ecdysis

i will shed this body that i hate
not by changing my appearance
she is staying
it is this cruel mind that has to leave
you have done enough
get out of this home

you are a moon with hands

when you feel joy
write a letter to your sad self
remind them of the sun
we all get trapped in torment
submerged by sadness
calmer versions do exist
the moon goes through phases too
but she is still whole
and holy just like you

you are an unfinished poem

with permission to add anything in ink
scratch out the part out of sync
with your heart

don't show me a neat piece of
perfect paper
skew lines, i prefer
handwritten highlighter

the mistakes and ripped edges
should always remain
for what is a great story without a coffee stain?

your magic has reached its full capacity

you are a tree with eyes
a cloud without skies
yet floating like a honeybee
the mixture of sun and sea
everything you dream
moonbeam
mythic with ice powers
your hair is simply flowers
that never die
even gold will drip when you cry
hold on to your constellations
you don't need renovations
as love and earth
the epitome of worth

moonlight magic

walking the path of lover's lane
i thank the mundane
the little things and how it sings
a soft but secure tune
we always have the moon
and flowers teach us their moves
the wind also soothes
wiggle with the trees
bewitched by a breeze
believe the ordinary to be a gift
and life will dream, and *shift*, and drift

sunflowers all stare in the same direction

there is something so impeccably beautiful
in seeing a single flower brightly bloom
doing it alone
using a body as a home
it makes me want to scream
i am the only person who has always been there for
me
there is no need for fields of poppies
or towers of staring sunflowers
your roots are deep below
trust yourself
the lonesome can also grow

looks like i'm flying

it breaks my heart to know how easily things can change
and here we are again
or here i am with myself and the wind
some of the most beautiful sunsets have been seen from a
  car ride home
while driving alone
i love being a mess
who should i impress
i don't run after you anymore,
you're on the ground
and i soar

heal before we can dance together

it is okay that you do not know how to heal
but you cannot break me today
i am an ocean away, or better yet
i am part sea, stay away from my restored body
or mend, i will lend you the remedy to become whole
you are enough
now feel it in your soul,
be a home, be a tree, and only then
can you come with me

your heart is talking to you

trust yourself, your heart wants to keep
  you safe
that intuition that keeps on whispering
  wishes and warnings
is something to consider, don't shrivel
  and wither away from your power
when you trust and love yourself, your
  taste will change
standards will raise
listen
your heartbeat is talking

a poem for my voice

i wrote a poem for my voice today
husky and sore after a weekend away
a weekend of screams
the good kind
painted in dreams
i am thankful for stories
and speaking in colour
you make me tough
rising from my throat, you remind me that i matter
my words are important
my voice is the only validation i require
my voice will inspire
because speaking up for myself is the most beautiful thing i
  can do
you proved that i am free
and there is nothing more liberating than having me

my dear body

this body is mine
carrying me to places
let me hold you with dear desire and hope to inspire others
  to do the same
you have a name
i will protect us
sorry for all the times that i have failed
when we did not want to be unveiled
all we can do is protect the young
my children, daughter, and my son

this body is yours
celebrate it, in every way
demand to have the final say
you belong in this skin
your body is not sin
no, it has always been
made of miracles

we live inside bones, yes we are homes

i have accepted being lost for so long
uncertainty rooted in my heart's song
she knows the lyrics
nothing but hysterics in words
strung together like pearls
i don't fear being lost or floating
my life is not loading, it is happening
as i sing, as we speak
as i seek
living homelessly not hopelessly
chasing wind and waves
leading to caves and back to my heart
once more
where adventure is boiling
i live in my core

i have studied the light
it always brings me back to you

chapter six

Two Trees Intertwined

the love poems

nature taught me how to love

be, and flow, and drift, and go,
and tree
two trees next to each other
how they bind and intertwine
separately as one
moon and sun
we run like rivers
kissing as the wind shivers
love like the waves
licking sand
a love that stars can understand
i called you love
and you turned around
i am happy you know your name

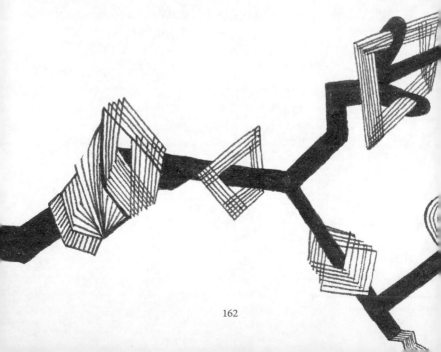

even if you aren't ready for love
love is ready for you

come swim in the sea with me

when i am with you
time does not exist
everything is pink light
green bright
we swim for hours and life unfolds
it feels good by your side
enjoy the ride
i am
look, we can breathe underwater
or perhaps we have been in the sky all along
if hearts could speak
our love would be a song

come with me to uncertainty

will you hold my hand and allow me to lead you to a place of
   uncertainty
it will always be filled with wonder
i don't know where we are going but i need your trust as fuel
our adventure has one rule
we must grow
it is a give and take
open your eyes along the way
this is what life feels like
being scared is a good thing
living is risky
sink into uncertainty
with me

you make me feel smart
i don't have a problem if you steal my heart

new love

we all have new love expectations
and i understand why we have them
but for reasons only blankets can understand
i will not be sharing my darkness yet
nothing to worry about
i don't drink blood,
or sing all the time
only most of the time
i can give you my music, and in the subway you can sit across
  from me
i sketch silhouettes quickly
rather messy but you look like a fine muse
and if i am being honest, when i fall in love
i drown, there is nothing gentle about my love
i don't count in halves or leave bites of crème brûlée
and your eyes, seem like a fine place to stay

i do not need you, but i want you

i do not need you
being wrapped in your arms is my meditation
i do not need you
we brush lips and i taste salvation
i do not need you
with binding bodies i become addicted to the way we feel
when you speak you make me heal
by touching you i become a star
i do not need you
but let me be wherever you are

**you are a masterpiece mixture of
messy, dark, and beautiful**

i assume you were birthed part moon
perhaps part sky
there is not a moment i don't want you by my side
silent, comfortably
my company eternally
who brightens each moment bitingly beautiful
your wit is sharper than the stars
the kind we drew with pencil in palms
as kids, the pages were filled with them
now we are women of the universe
through space and time we can immerse
expansive
it truly is a victory
to have you
right here
next to me

okay heart, you need to calm down right now

dear heart,
crimson life force
stop skipping so many beats
for a handsome boy who speaks
people are searching for drums
keep the thumping thunder under control
he stole more than a grin
i know you cannot take him in enough
it is rough to lose your mind
but focus on something else
like yourself
restack the bookshelf
anything
stop thinking about him

mornings

you give me something to hold
  on to
as we wake up
like ivy
turning into cursive
i look at you and see ladybugs on
  your cheeks
we sink through these sheets
my *smile*
stay forever if you like

happy with you

you made me sing today
those happy eyes
gorgeously glistening
made me sing
without asking
only smirks and dimples necessary

words of affirmation

do you love me?
i ask again trying to sound less begging
than five minutes ago
hoping your "yes" will carry the truth i couldn't detect the
  previous twelve times
your eyes now carry sadness
and hopeless hands flop in questioning like you are mocking
  an angel
who made you like this?
you ask
the question triggering a tucked away feeling
abandonment is still there
much alive holding hands with betrayal
i don't know how to let them die, they seem to be
  procreating
you cup my cheeks with palms
extreme eye contact now follows
and after excessive heavy breathing
i love you

a letter to the future love of my life

i am not sure if we have met but
you are going to hold me uncomfortably long
sinking into arms warm
this heart of mine is delicate
butterfly fragile
i know your smile will melt my legs
and my lips will beg for endless kisses
there is never a clear time to terminate touch
affection is a pretty fine love language
sublime,
i can't wait to call you mine and to
recruit you as my muse
all this i feel even before
i know your name
our future feels limitless
and this is the hope i carry,
with love,
the woman you'll marry

you belong to you, but i'd like it if you stayed

sorry to be sentimental
i have nothing holy
only holding on to memories
of places
how i experience spaces
owning books and a car
but do not possess people
myself
yes
you are free to leave my side
forever terrified
choose to stay
is the only thing i bear to say
my love
no
we are simply birds with human faces

we can both be stars

we do not have forever
my love
return to me
my dream, we are part sea
your fingers in my hair
as we become one
the sun is a star yes
i'll follow your caress
we do not have forever
i'll spend it on your chest
do not slip away
rather be my day

my arms are open
to receive you
to breathe you

meet my soul

i live in this heart
deeply,
darkly, darling see
me in front of you
this vulnerability is,
i keep saying
i keep replaying, in a way
praying
to not be afraid
i may push you away
if you leave

it's okay

being open should not be a deal breaker
being chaotic and feeling too much
feeling everything, feeling the world
is not something i am able to hide
if you stay by my side
me, wild with sensitivity,
and choose to hold this whole ocean admiring, star firing–
    thing
i may start to cling but i'll always sing the songs you love as
    well
if i get to tell you what lives in my soul when the night feels
    like forever
then darling, there is nowhere i'd rather be, than together

how to become love

step 1: study the sun not by staring
but feeling

step 2: generate heat from the belly
and blow on your fingers
when you don't need gloves
anymore you can start practising
on potential suitors,
if they turn it down do not apologise
simply say, "i am learning to become
love" and prance away like a zebra

step 3: offer gum to a stranger
once every month

step 4: tell the moon your deepest secrets and ask
her for wings
when she says no and unfortunately she
will say no
say thank you three times and
start laughing

step 5: kindly ask the ocean to baptise your new body and
turn it into love
the ocean likes the cleansing process, it knows that a small
piece of your dna becomes sand which will be used for
sandcastles and mermaid tails

the ocean giggles and foam drools from his mouth,
"you are love" says the ocean "but the best part is you can have
it too"

a very serious love poem

we can watch the moon together and you can fall asleep on
  my shoulder
forever
this is something i propose
my hair makes a puffy pillow, but they tend to scratch the
  nose
you have the most adorable sneeze so forgive me if there is a
  purposeful prickle
keep your finger away from my belly i hate that tickle
rather bat one eyelash next to my jaw
you dream like a cat and i don't mind if you snore
i like hearing you
i like feeling you
don't make me stop holding
when i feel you unfolding i pause my breath
i think loving you will be my death

love poems

the title with the most competition
comparing you to
the moon, the sun, the beaches,
all that blooms,
stars,
the smell of my childhood
and most recently:
charcuterie boards
the list goes on
an endless song
of kisses and licks and bites
exclaiming how i may die
if we were to part
how my heart will drown a thousand deaths
in its own blood
a flood of cries
the sea where my soul dies

love poems

what have you done to us?

i will have time for you

my darling
i will have time for you to encompass
the surrounding that is me
trace every part of this venus body
breathing you into
all of my existence
till the sun says goodbye
moons falling from sky
and the stars collapse
loving you,
is my climax

vows are sexy

be my forever
you swear,
i swear
nothing sounds more delicious than that

becoming love

and when we become love
we realise it is only acceptance
how we carry it along with each moment of our lives
as we step out of the ocean
as we wink at the sun
as we trace the rain over our arms
rubbing fragrance into palms
love with intention
with warmth
and overwhelming kindness
hold every hand you find
and soon the flowers
will grow from your mind

i was not ready for love
but love was clearly ready for me

there is a war in my mind and i love you

endless *i am okay*s said smoothly without a blink, a croak
or a crack to make you think, nothing is amiss
this "i am fine" sense of self has reached its maximum
  capacity
my deceitful normality
has passed many tests
but i have overextended the parts of me
and dishonesty cannot make a home here
any longer

i am sorry
i don't know what to say
i am so sorry
i am not okay

kissing you

my dry lips have a gift
they create a voluptuous kiss
come here
a prickly pear has tough skin
but the sweetness within inspires
wonder
limitless with touch
feeling too much for ordinary souls
made of stars and a hint of chance
my mouth can dance
and i found the one
who can handle this sun

thank you for being gentle with my heart

i love you, i love you

we said i love you for the first time and i felt honesty
meant to be
honestly
i want to blurt it out, every chance i get
i think our hearts just met
i love you
i love you
but i can't be a waterfall with words
too scared that every time i say it, the meaning becomes less
  valuable
don't let them go to waste
the taste is too sweet
too good
this life is a dance with you
hold my hands
yes both
and like an oath
i will be here
to make the skies a little more clear
'cause running in the rain with you
will always be my perfect view

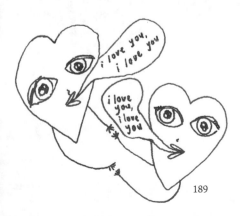

write love poems to your friends

my friend asked me if i can write a
  poem about her
i answered of course
she said it has to be the most
  beautiful poem to ever reach the
  stars
and i told her
you already are

i want you there

you worship these thighs
and i sink into your eyes
please stare,
i want you
everywhere

and if i fall in love with you

may the pool be as cool as your hazel eyes
may we hold soft skin and breathe in the skies
if i fall
let it be lukewarm
like your touch
may we always love too much
i want to understand
every inch of your mind
a galaxy of treasure
who knows what i'll find
may you listen to me
all this talk of the sea
and the way my brain jumps from deep under to star high
if we fall in love
make it never die

ocean beings

i have held with tender
my body in surrender
give me all
the bad and the gold
these hands,
only two
but for you
is shaped like a ship
your quivering underlip
can speak without thinking
secrets are for *sinking*
lay the heavy on me
and just like that
we resemble the sea

where did you come from?

it is real, my love
the wonderful simplicity of us, as we move smoothly and
  slow
there is no rush
you are the destination
this moment is adventure
when did you become the center of my world?
gold and tender in all your splendor
forever finding my calm in your arms and gaze
i'll freeze the days to make them last
don't go fast
only kiss me again
i'll tell you to stop
when i say when

reveal the sea seals

let me lie in the sand
rolling and rubbing silky bodies
thank you for joining me today
we will probably turn into seals
laughing with you hurts my tummy
yes, i am grabbing your face
you are my favourite animal
i am drawn to you
please don't stop me from following you into the sea
i want to be where you are
when we die
we'll be the same star

my chimera cuddly man

next to you
is an interesting mix of eternal comfort
and gasping for air
each time i drown in your eyes
i realise i can breathe you in
cuddling like a little sloth next to you
we made a cocoon
and look,
 you make me swoon

my perfect night

you tell me you like the planets in my eyes
and i become the moon you manifested
when you made me feel like venus
bodies are swaying
giggling as if we have a secret
tonight we are dolphins
and it is thrilling to be an adult with you

damn baby i really love you

how gorgeous it is to write
especially when my subject matter is you
the only thing i would rather be doing, is be with you all the
  time
i cannot believe you are mine
let me take care of you
we have begun
this cannot be undone
the story of us will tumble forward
i cannot believe i get to kiss you
there is going to be a lot of love poems about you
my *darling*
i love you
i love you a lot
warmer than the sun
i know you are the one

the end

future poem

here you are
in front of a poetess
blank
sky-like
asking her to be brave
to pour on you
paper and rain do not go well together

i write because it gives me a clear way to communicate
poetry amplifies my voice
i do not try and live in a daydream
but i do try and limit the amount of hate in this world
especially self hate,
there is no point in being your own worst enemy
we talk to ourselves in such damaging ways
work on loving yourself
with all your funky flaws
appreciate this life
there are so many adventures waiting for you
let go of the judgment
it will make you free

Christi Steyn was born in South Africa, where she studied English, theater, and education. She is an avid lover of the ocean, impulsive dance sessions, and conversations with the mountains. Having amassed millions of followers worldwide for her captivating readings of poetry, Christi hopes to make her readers fall in love with words. She believes in adventure, the beauty of storytelling, and hopes to continue to connect with readers through poetry.

Instagram: christi.steyn
TikTok: christi.steyn